JAVASCRIPT Programming Guide for Beginners

STEP BY STEP

ISAAC WILLIAMS

Copyright © 2024 Isaac Williams

Todos los derechos reservados.

DEDICATION

I dedicate this book to all readers, both those who are taking their first steps in the world of programming and those who continue to learn and grow. May these pages be the beginning of an exciting journey towards mastering JavaScript and software development.

Dedication

CONTENT

INTRODUCTION 1
CHAPTER 1: INTRODUCTION TO PROGRAMMING WITH PSEUDOCODE 4
CHAPTER 2: FUNDAMENTALS OF PROGRAMMING IN JAVASCRIPT 10
CHAPTER 3: FLOW CONTROL 17
CHAPTER 4: FUNCTIONS 22
CHAPTER 5: DATA STRUCTURES 28
CHAPTER 6: DOM MANIPULATION 33
CHAPTER 7: ADVANCED FEATURES OF ES6 40
CHAPTER 8: OBJECT-ORIENTED PROGRAMMING IN JAVASCRIPT 47
CHAPTER 9: SMALL PROJECTS 53
CHAPTER 10: DEBUGGING AND BEST PRACTICES 68
CHAPTER 11: PUBLISHING AND DEPLOYMENT 76
CHAPTER 12: EXPLORING JAVASCRIPT FRAMEWORKS 80
APPENDIX: PRACTICAL EXERCISES 89
GLOSSARY 92

ACKNOWLEDGMENTS

I want to express my sincere gratitude to all the people who have been part of this journey towards the creation of this book. To those who inspired me from the beginning and believed in me, to the mentors, colleagues, and friends who shared their wisdom and support, and to my family for their unconditional love. I also thank the readers for choosing to explore these pages and I hope they find inspiration and learning in this journey through the world of programming. Thank you all for being part of this exciting project!

INTRODUCTION

What is programming?

Imagine programming as giving instructions to a computer to perform specific tasks. It's like teaching a robot what to do. Instead of using human words, we use a programming language like JavaScript that the computer can understand.

Why learn JavaScript?

JavaScript is one of the most popular and versatile programming languages. It's mainly used for creating interactive websites. With JavaScript, you can make buttons change color when hovered over, create forms that validate user-entered information, and much more. It's an excellent starting point for learning to program.

Required Tools

Before diving into writing JavaScript code, you'll need some basic tools:

Code Editors

A code editor is like a notebook where you'll write your JavaScript instructions. Some popular editors include:

- **Visual Studio Code:** It's free, user-friendly, and packed with useful features for beginner programmers.

- **Atom:** Another popular and user-friendly editor.

Browsers

Browsers are like windows through which we'll see the results of our JavaScript code. Some common browsers include:

- Google Chrome
- Mozilla Firefox
- Microsoft Edge

Browser Console

The console is a tool within the browser that allows us to view messages and errors that occur when running our code. It's useful for debugging and understanding what's happening. To open the console:

- **In Chrome:** Right-click on the web page, select "Inspect," and go to the "Console" tab.

- **In Firefox:** Right-click and select "Inspect Element," then go to the "Console" tab.

Practice: Hello World in JavaScript

Before delving deeper, let's write our first program in JavaScript: the classic "Hello World." This will help us get familiar with the syntax and see how a simple program is executed.

To write "Hello World" in JavaScript, follow these steps:

1. Open your code editor (e.g., Visual Studio Code).

2. Create a new file and save it with the name hello-world.js.

3. Write the following code in the file:

```javascript
console.log("Hello World");
```

4. Save the file.

5. Open your browser and navigate to the page where you have the hello-world.js file.

6. Open the browser console to see the result. You should see "Hello World" printed in the console.

Congratulations! You've written and executed your first program in JavaScript.

CHAPTER 1: INTRODUCTION TO PROGRAMMING WITH PSEUDOCODE

We'll start from the basics, understanding the fundamental concepts of programming, and gradually advance through practical examples in pseudocode. Get ready to explore the essential pillars of programming and delve into problem-solving step by step.

What is Programming?

Programming is the process of creating instructions that tell a computer how to perform a specific task. These instructions are written in programming languages and can address a wide range of problems, from simple calculations to managing complex systems.

Pseudocode

Pseudocode is an informal language used to describe algorithms in a clear and readable way. Unlike real programming languages, pseudocode does not have strict syntax and can be expressed in various forms.

Fundamental Concepts

Algorithm

An algorithm is a finite sequence of well-defined steps that solves a specific problem. It's like a recipe that follows a series of steps to achieve a desired result.

Variables

Variables are data containers that can store values and change during program execution. Let's see how to define variables and what we can do with them in pseudocode:

Variable Definition:

Variables are defined by specifying the data type and variable name. Here's an example of how to define an integer variable and assign it a value:

```pseudocódigo
Integer age = 25
```

In this example, we have defined a variable called age that contains a value of 25.

Using Variables:

Variables can be used to store values and perform calculations. For example, we can use variables to perform simple arithmetic operations:

```
pseudocódigo

Start
    // Define variables
    Integer number1 = 10
    Integer number2 = 5
    Integer sum, subtract, multiplication, division

    // Perform arithmetic operations
    sum = number1 + number2
    subtract = number1 - number2
    multiplication = number1 * number2
    division = number1 / number2

    // Show results
    Write "The sum is:", sum
    Write "The subtraction is:", subtract
    Write "The multiplication is:", multiplication
    Write "The division is:", division
End
```

In this example, we have defined variables to store two numbers (number1 and number2) and then performed various arithmetic operations using those variables.

Conditionals

Conditionals are control structures that allow a program to make decisions based on certain conditions. Let's see a simple example of how to use conditionals in pseudocode to determine if a number entered by the user is positive, negative, or equal to zero:

```
pseudocode
Start
    // Define variable to store the number
    Integer number

    // Ask the user to input a number
    Write "Enter a number:"
    Read number

    // Check if the number is positive, negative, or equal to zero
    If number > 0 then
        Write "The number is positive."
    End If

    If number < 0 then
        Write "The number is negative."
    End If

    If number == 0 then
        Write "The number is equal to zero."
    End If
End
```

In this example, we use the If structure to check three different conditions:

- If the number is greater than 0, we print "The number is positive."

- If the number is less than 0, we print "The number is negative."

- If none of the above conditions are met, it means the number is equal to 0, so we print "The number is equal to zero."

Loops

Loops are control structures that allow a program to repeat a series of instructions multiple times. For example, "repeat this task until a condition is met."

Example of For Loop:

```pseudocode
Start
    // Define variable for the sum
    Integer sum = 0

    // Repeat the loop 5 times
    For Integer i = 1 to 5 with step 1 do
        // Add the value of i to the sum
        sum = sum + i
    End For

    // Show the result
    Write "The sum is:", sum
End
```

In this example, the For loop is repeated 5 times, adding the values of i to the variable sum in each iteration.

Practice with Pseudocode

Now, I invite you to practice by writing your own pseudocode to solve simple problems, such as calculating the area of a triangle or determining if a number is even or odd. Use the fundamental concepts of programming we just learned and express your solutions clearly and logically.

Conclusions

Pseudocode is an excellent way to familiarize yourself with the basic concepts of programming before diving into a real programming language.

CHAPTER 2: FUNDAMENTALS OF PROGRAMMING IN JAVASCRIPT

Basic Concepts

In this section, we will explore some basic concepts of programming that will help you better understand how JavaScript works.

Variables

Variables are like boxes where you can store information to use later in your program. For example, imagine a box called "name" where you can store a person's name. In JavaScript, you can create a variable like this:

```javascript
let name;
```

Here, let is a keyword that tells JavaScript you are creating a variable called "name".

After the = sign, you can assign it a value:

```javascript
let name = "Juan";
```

Now, the variable "name" contains the value "Juan".

Data Types

In JavaScript, there are several data types you can store in variables:

- **Numbers:** such as 5, 10.5, etc.

- **Strings:** such as "Hello", "JavaScript", etc. They always go in quotes (" or ').

- **Booleans:** true or false, representing true or false.

- **Null and Undefined:** representing null or undefined values.

Operators

Operators in JavaScript are symbols used to perform operations on variables and values. Some basic operators are:

- **Arithmetic:** + (addition), - (subtraction), * (multiplication), / (division).

- **Assignment:** = (assigns a value to a variable).

- **Comparison:** === (strict equality), !== (strict

inequality), > (greater than), < (less than), etc.

- **Logical:** && (logical AND), || (logical OR), ! (logical NOT).

Comments

Comments are texts you can include in your code to make it more readable and explain what you're doing. In JavaScript, you can use **//** for single-line comments and **/* */** for multi-line comments:

```javascript
// This is a single-line comment

/*
This is a
multi-line comment
*/
```

Practice: Creating and Using Variables

Let's practice by creating some variables and performing basic operations with them:

1. Open your code editor.
2. Create a new file and save it as variables.js.

3. Write the following code:

```javascript
// Create variables
let number = 5;
let name = "Maria";
let isTrue = true;

// Display variables in the console
console.log(number); // You should see 5
console.log(name); // You should see "Maria"
console.log(isTrue); // You should see true

// Perform operations
let sum = number + 10;
console.log(sum); // You should see 15

let message = "Hello, " + name;
console.log(message); // You should see "Hello, Maria"
```

4. Save the file and open it in your browser.

5. Open the browser console to see the results of the operations we performed.

Getting Started with JavaScript

What is the console and why is it important?

The browser console is a vital tool for web developers. It allows us to see messages, errors, and results of our JavaScript code. It's like a window to communicate with our web page.

To open the console:

1. In Google Chrome: Right-click on the web page, select "Inspect," and go to the "Console" tab.

2. In Mozilla Firefox: Right-click and select "Inspect Element," then go to the "Console" tab.

3. Displaying messages with console.log()

console.log() is a function in JavaScript that allows us to print messages to the browser console. It's useful for checking if our code is working as expected.

Let's print a greeting message to the console:

1. Open your code editor.

2. Create a new HTML file and save it as index.html.

3. Write the following basic HTML code:

```html
<!DOCTYPE html>
<html lang="en">
<head>
   <meta charset="UTF-8">
   <title>My First page with JavaScript</title>
</head>
<body>
   <h1>My First page with JavaScript</h1>

   <script>
      console.log("¡Hello from JavaScript!");
```

```
    </script>
  </body>
</html>
```

4. Save the file and open it in your browser.

5. Open the browser console to see the printed message.

Using alert() and prompt()

alert() and prompt() are two built-in functions in JavaScript that allow us to interact with the user.

- **alert()**: Displays an alert message in a popup window.

- **prompt()**: Displays a message and waits for the user to input something.

Let's see an example of each one:

```html
<script>
  // Alert
  alert("Hello from an alert!");

  // Prompt
  let name = prompt("Please enter your name:");
  console.log("The entered name is: " + name);
</script>
```

When you open the page in your browser, you'll first see the alert and then you'll be able to input your name in the prompt. The name you input will be shown in the console.

Practice: Your Turn!

Now it's your chance to practice. In the same index.html file, add the following below the previous code:

```html
<script>
// Write your own code here
</script>
```

You can try creating variables, performing simple mathematical operations, displaying messages with console.log(), alert(), or prompt(). Be creative and have fun!

Conclusion

In this section, we've learned the first steps with JavaScript:

- We used console.log() to display messages in the console.

- We explored alert() and prompt() to interact with the user.

- We practiced writing our own JavaScript code on a web page.

CHAPTER 3: FLOW CONTROL

In this chapter, we'll learn about flow control in JavaScript. This allows us to make decisions in our code and repeat tasks as needed.

Conditionals

Conditionals are code blocks that execute only if a specific condition is met. In JavaScript, we use the keywords if, else if, and else to create conditionals.

if, else if, and else:

```javascript
let age = 18;

if (age < 18) {
    console.log("You are underage");
```

```
} else if (age === 18) {
  console.log("You are 18 years old");
} else {
  console.log("You are of legal age");
}
```

In this example:

- If the age is less than 18, "You are under age" will be printed.

- If the age is exactly 18, "You are 18 years old" will be printed.

- Otherwise, "You are of legal age" will be printed.

Logical Operators

Logical operators allow us to combine multiple conditions into a single conditional.

- **&& (logical AND)**: Satisfied if both conditions are true.

- **|| (logical OR)**: Satisfied if at least one of the conditions is true.

- **! (logical NOT)**: Negates a condition.

Example with && (logical AND)

```javascript
let isAdult = true;
let hasLicense = true;

if (isAdult && hasLicense) {
    console.log("Can drive");
} else {
    console.log("Cannot drive");
}
```

In this case, the person can drive only if they are an adult and have a license.

Loops

Loops allow us to repeat a task multiple times. In JavaScript, we have the for, while, and do...while loops.

for Loop

The for loop is used when we know exactly how many times we want to repeat a task.

```javascript
for (let i = 1; i <= 5; i++) {
    console.log("Number: " + i);
}
```

This loop will print numbers from 1 to 5.

while Loop

The while loop is used when we want to repeat a task as long as a condition is met.

```javascript
let counter = 0;
while (counter < 3) {
    console.log("Counter: " + counter);
    counter++;
}
```

This loop will print the counter from 0 to 2.

do...while Loop

The do...while loop is similar to while, but ensures that the task is executed at least once before checking the condition.

```javascript
let x = 1;
do {
    console.log("Number: " + x);
    x++;
} while (x <= 3);
```

This loop will print numbers from 1 to 3.

Practice

Now it's your turn to practice. Use what you've learned to write code that:

1. Checks if a number is even or odd.

2. Repeats a phrase 5 times.

3. Finds the sum of numbers from 1 to 10.

Feel free to try different combinations of conditionals and loops for more practice. Remember to use console.log() to see the results in the browser console.

Conclusion

In this chapter, we've learned about flow control in JavaScript:

- We used conditionals (if, else if, else) to make decisions based on conditions.

- Explored logical operators (&&, ||, !) to combine conditions.

- Learned about loops (for, while, do...while) to repeat tasks as needed.

CHAPTER 4: FUNCTIONS

What Are Functions?

Imagine a function as a machine that takes something (inputs or arguments), performs a specific task with it, and then may return something (output or return). Functions allow us to write code that we can use over and over again without having to repeat it.

Function Declaration

In JavaScript, we can declare a function like this:

```javascript
function greet() {
   console.log("¡Hello!");
}
```

In this example, we've declared a function called greet that simply prints "Hello!" to the console.

Calling a Function

To use a function, we simply call it by its name:

```javascript
greet(); // This will print "Hello!" to the console
```

When we call greet(), the code inside the function executes, and we see "Hello!" printed to the console.

Parameters and Arguments

Functions can accept information passed to them, called parameters. We can think of parameters as internal variables of the function that we use to perform specific tasks.

Example with Parameters

```javascript
function greetPerson(name) {
   console.log("Hello, " + name + "!");
}

greetPerson("Juan"); // "Hello, Juan!" in the console
greetPerson("Maria"); // "Hello, Maria!" in the console
```

In this case, name is a parameter of the greetPerson function. When we call the function with a specific name, that name is used inside the function to generate a personalized greeting.

Returning Values

Functions can return a result after performing their task. We use the return keyword to specify the value the function should return.

Example with Return

```javascript
function sum(a, b) {
    let result = a + b;
    return result;
}

let total = sum(5, 3);
console.log(total); // This will print 8 to the console
```

In this example, the sum function takes two numbers as arguments (a and b), adds them together, and then returns the result. We then store that result in the variable total and display it in the console.

Variable Scope

Variables inside a function have local scope. This means they only exist within the function and are not accessible from outside of it.

Scope Example

```javascript
function multiplyByTwo(number) {
   let result = number * 2;
   return result;
}

console.log(result); // This will give an error, as result is not defined here
```

In this case, result is a local variable of the doubleByTwo function and cannot be accessed outside of the function.

Anonymous Functions and Arrow Functions

In addition to traditional functions, JavaScript also has anonymous functions and arrow functions, which are more compact ways to write functions.

Anonymous Function

```javascript
let greet = function() {
   console.log("Hello from anonymous function!");
};
greet(); // This will print "Hello from anonymous function!" to the console
```

Arrow Function

```javascript
let greet = () => {
    console.log("Hello from arrow function!");
};
greet(); // This will print "Hello from arrow function!" to the console
```

Arrow functions are especially useful when we want a shorter and clearer syntax.

Practice: Creating and Using Functions

Now it's your turn to practice. Use what you've learned to write and use functions:

- Create a function called square that takes a number as an argument and returns its square.

- Create a function called greetName that takes a name as an argument and returns a personalized greeting.

- Use these functions with different values and display the results in the console.

Conclusion

In this chapter, we've explored functions in JavaScript:

- Learned what functions are and how to declare them.

- Saw how to pass parameters to functions and use them inside.

- Understood the concept of returning values and the scope of variables within functions.

- Explored anonymous functions and arrow functions as alternative ways to write functions.

CHAPTER 5: DATA STRUCTURES

Arrays

An array is an ordered collection of elements. You can think of an array as a list of elements, where each element has a numerical position called an index. In JavaScript, arrays can contain any type of data, including numbers, strings, other arrays, objects, and more.

Creating Arrays

```javascript
let numbers = [1, 2, 3, 4, 5];
let fruits = ["Apple", "Banana", "Cherry"];
let mixed = [1, "two", true];
```

In these examples, we have created arrays with numbers, strings, and a mix of different data types.

Accessing Elements

To access a specific element in an array, we use its index. The first element has index 0, the second index 1, and so on.

```javascript
console.log(numbers[0]); // This will print 1
console.log(fruits[1]); // This will print "Banana"
```

Modifying Elements

We can modify the elements of an array by assigning a new value to its index.

```javascript
fruits[0] = "Orange";
console.log(fruits); // This will print ["Orange", "Banana", "Cherry"]
```

Array Methods

JavaScript provides many useful methods for working with arrays. Some common examples are:

- push(): Adds a new element to the end of the array.

- pop(): Removes the last element from the array.

- splice(): Allows deleting, replacing, or adding elements at specific positions in the array.

Objects

An object is a collection of key-value pairs. Each value in an object is associated with a unique key. This allows us to organize information in a more structured and descriptive way.

Creating Objects

```javascript
let person = {
  name: "Juan",
  age: 25,
  city: "Madrid"
};
```

In this example, we have created an object person with three properties: name, age, and city.

Accessing Properties

We can access the properties of an object using dot notation (.) or bracket notation ([]).

```javascript
console.log(person.name); // This will print "Juan"
console.log(person["age"]); // This will print 25
```

Modifying Properties

We can modify the properties of an object in the same way as the elements of an array.

```javascript
person.age = 30;
console.log(person); // This will print { name: "Juan", age: 30, city: "Madrid" }
```

Practice with Arrays and Objects

Now it's your turn to practice with arrays and objects:

- Create an array called numbers with some numbers.

- Create an object called car with properties such as brand, model, and year.

- Access elements of the array and properties of the object.

- Modify elements of the array and properties of the object.

- Try out some array methods like push() and splice().

- Experiment with different data types in arrays and objects.

Conclusion

In this chapter, we explored data structures in JavaScript:

- Learned about arrays and how to store and access elements in them.

- Explored objects and how they represent collections of key-value pairs.

- Practiced creating, accessing, and modifying arrays and objects.

CHAPTER 6: DOM MANIPULATION

What is the DOM?

The DOM is a structured representation of an HTML document that the browser can understand and manipulate. Each element on a web page, such as texts, images, buttons, etc., is a node in the DOM tree.

Element Selection

We can select elements from the DOM using methods like getElementById(), getElementsByClassName(), getElementsByTagName(), and querySelector().

getElementById()

This method selects an element by its unique ID.

```html
<!DOCTYPE html>
<html>
<head>
  <title>Selecting Elements</title>
</head>
<body>
  <h1 id="titulo">Welcome</h1>
  <p>This is a sample paragraph.</p>

  <script>
    let title = document.getElementById("titulo");
    console.log(title); // This will display the <h1 id="titulo"> element in the console
  </script>
</body>
</html>
```

getElementsByClassName()

This method selects elements by their class.

```html
<!DOCTYPE html>
<html>
<head>
  <title>Selecting Elements</title>
</head>
<body>
  <ul>
    <li class="item">Element 1</li>
    <li class="item">Element 2</li>
```

```html
    <li class="item">Element 3</li>
  </ul>

  <script>
    let items = document.getElementsByClassName("item");
    console.log(items); // This will display a list of elements with the class "item" in the console
  </script>
</body>
</html>
```

getElementsByTagName()

This method selects elements by their tag.

```html
<!DOCTYPE html>
<html>
<head>
  <title>Selecting Elements</title>
</head>
<body>
  <ul>
    <li>Element 1</li>
    <li>Element 2</li>
    <li>Element 3</li>
  </ul>
  <script>
    let listItems = document.getElementsByTagName("li");
    console.log(listItems);
  </script>
</body>
</html>
```

querySelector()

This method allows selecting elements using CSS selectors.

```html
<!DOCTYPE html>
<html>
<head>
  <title>Selecting Elements</title>
</head>
<body>
  <div id="container">
    <p class="paragraph">This is a paragraph.</p>
    <p class="paragraph">This is another paragraph.</p>
  </div>

  <script>
    let paragraph = document.querySelector(".paragraph");
    console.log(paragraph);
  </script>
</body>
</html>
```

Content Manipulation

Once we have selected an element from the DOM, we can change its content using the innerHTML and textContent properties.

innerHTML

The innerHTML property allows getting or setting the HTML

content of an element.

```javascript
let paragraph = document.getElementById("paragraph");
paragraph.innerHTML = "<strong>New Content</strong>";
```

textContent

The textContent property allows getting or setting only the text content in an element.

```javascript
let title = document.getElementById("title");
title.textContent = "New Title";
```

Style Manipulation

We can also modify the CSS styles of an element using the style property.

Change Background Color

```javascript
let paragraph = document.getElementById("paragraph");
paragraph.style.backgroundColor = "yellow";
```

Change Font Size

```javascript
let title = document.getElementById("title");
title.style.fontSize = "24px";
```

Events

Events are actions that occur on the webpage, such as clicking a button, moving the mouse over an element, etc. We can assign functions to execute when these events occur.

Click Event

```html
<!DOCTYPE html>
<html>
<head>
    <title>Events</title>
</head>
<body>
    <button id="boton">Click here</button>

    <script>
        let button = document.getElementById("button");
        button.addEventListener("click", function() {
            alert("¡Button Clicked!");
        });
    </script>
</body>
</html>
```

In this example, we have assigned a function to display an alert when the button is clicked.

Practice: DOM Manipulation

Now it's your turn to practice DOM manipulation:

- Select an element from your webpage using one of the methods seen.

- Change its content using innerHTML or textContent.

- Modify some CSS styles of the element using the style property.

- Assign an event to an element to trigger something to happen when an action occurs, such as clicking a button.

Conclusion

In this chapter, we have learned about DOM manipulation in JavaScript:

- We learned to select elements from the DOM using different methods.

- Explored how to change the content and styles of elements.

- Assigned events to elements to execute functions when actions occur on the webpage.

CHAPTER 7: ADVANCED FEATURES OF ES6

In this chapter, we will explore some of the more advanced features introduced in ECMAScript 6 (also known as ES6), which is a significant version of JavaScript released in 2015.

These features make writing JavaScript code easier, more concise, and more powerful.

Let and Const

ES6 introduced let and const as new ways to declare variables, which have a stricter block scope than var.

LET

Let is used to declare variables that can change in value.

```javascript
let nombre = "Juan";
nombre = "María"; // This is valid
```

CONST

Const is used to declare constants, whose value cannot change once assigned.

```javascript
const PI = 3.1416;
// PI = 3; //Will throw an error, constants cannot be reassigned
```

Arrow Functions

Arrow functions are a more concise way to write functions in JavaScript, with simpler syntax and a different behavior for this.

Basic Syntax

```javascript
// Traditional function
function sum(a, b) {
    return a + b;
}
// Arrow function
let sum = (a, b) => a + b;
```

With Parameters and Block Body

```javascript
// Arrow function with parameters
let square = (x) => x * x;

// Arrow function with block body
let square = (x) => {
   return x * x;
};
```

this in Arrow Functions

In arrow functions, this refers to the lexical context in which the function is defined, rather than the object calling the function.

```javascript
let person = {
   name: "Juan",
   greet: function() {
      setTimeout(function() {
         console.log("Hello, I am " + this.name);
// This will give an error, this is not the person
      }, 1000);
   }
};
person.greet();
```

To resolve this issue, we can use an arrow function:

```javascript
let person = {
  name: "Juan",
  greet: function() {
    setTimeout(() => {
      console.log("Hello, I am " + this.name);
// This will display "Hello, I am Juan"
    }, 1000);
  }
};
person.greet();
```

Template Strings

Template strings are a more convenient way to work with strings in JavaScript, allowing interpolation of variables and expressions.

Syntax

```javascript
let name = "Juan";
let age = 25;
let message = `Hello, my name is ${name} and I am ${age} years old.`;
console.log(message);
//"Hello, my name is Juan and I am 25 years old."
```

Destructuring

Destructuring is a way to extract values from arrays or objects and assign them to variables in a more compact way.

Array Destructuring

```javascript
let numbers = [1, 2, 3];
let [a, b, c] = numbers;
console.log(a); // This will display 1
console.log(b); // This will display 2
console.log(c); // This will display 3
```

Object Destructuring

```javascript
let person = {
  nombre: "María",
  edad: 30
};
let { nombre, edad } = person;
console.log(nombre); // This will display "María"
console.log(edad); // This will display 30
```

Default Parameters

ES6 allows defining default values for function parameters, which will be used if no value is provided when calling the function.

Syntax

```javascript
function greet(nombre = "User") {
   console.log("Hello, " + nombre);
}

greet(); // This will display "Hello, User"
greet("Juan"); // This will display "Hello, Juan"saludar();
```

Practice with ES6 Features

Now it's your turn to practice with the advanced features of ES6:

- Now it's your turn to practice with the advanced features of ES6:

- Use let and const to declare variables in your code.

- Create some arrow functions to perform simple tasks.

- Experiment with template strings to build text messages.

- Practice destructuring with arrays and objects.

- Define default parameters in some functions and observe their behavior.

Conclusion

In this chapter, we have explored some of the advanced features introduced in ECMAScript 6 (ES6):

- We learned about let and const to declare variables with block scope.

- We explored arrow functions as a more concise and clear way to write functions.

- We used template strings to work with text strings more conveniently.

- We practiced destructuring to extract values from arrays or objects more compactly.

- We saw how default parameters can be useful when defining functions.

CHAPTER 8: OBJECT-ORIENTED PROGRAMMING IN JAVASCRIPT

In this chapter, we will explore Object-Oriented Programming (OOP) in JavaScript. OOP is a programming paradigm based on the concept of "objects" that can contain data in the form of properties and functions in the form of methods.

We will learn how to create classes, objects, properties, methods, and how to work with inheritance in JavaScript.

What is Object-Oriented Programming?

OOP is a programming paradigm based on the concept of "objects," which are instances of "classes." A class is a model that defines the properties and methods common to a type of object.

Classes and Objects

In JavaScript, we can define a class using the class keyword.

```javascript
class Person {
  constructor(name, age) {
    this.name = name;
    this.age = age;
  }

  greet() {
    console.log(`Hello, I'm ${this.name} and I'm ${this.age} years old.`);
  }
}

// Creating an object of the Person class
let person1 = new Person("Juan", 30);
let person2 = new Person("María", 25);

person1.greet(); // "Hello, I'm Juan and I'm 30 years old."
person2.greet(); // "Hello, I'm María and I'm 25 years old."
```

In this example, Person is a class with properties name and age, and a method greet() that displays a message.

Constructors and Methods

The constructor method is a special method that is automatically called when an object of the class is created. It is where we initialize the object's properties.

```javascript
class Car {
  constructor(brand, model) {
    this.brand = brand;
    this.model = model;
  }

  showInfo() {
    console.log(`Car: ${this.brand} ${this.model}`);
  }
}

let car1 = new Car("Toyota", "Corolla");
car1.showInfo(); // "Car: Toyota Corolla"
```

Inheritance

In OOP, inheritance is a mechanism that allows us to create a new class based on an existing class. The new class inherits properties and methods from the base class.

Syntax of Inheritance

```javascript
class Animal {
  constructor(name) {
    this.name = name;
  }
  makeSound() {
    console.log("Making generic sound");
```

```
    }
  }

class Dog extends Animal {
    constructor(name, breed) {
        super(name); // Calls the base class constructor
        this.breed = breed;
    }

    makeSound() {
        console.log("Woof woof");
    }

    showInfo() {
        console.log(`Dog: ${this.name}, Breed: ${this.breed}`);
    }
}

let myDog = new Dog("Bobby", "Labrador");
myDog.showInfo(); // "Dog: Bobby, Breed: Labrador"
myDog.makeSound(); // "Woof woof"
```

In this example, Dog is a class that inherits from the Animal class. Dog has its own constructor and makeSound() method, but it can also access the properties and methods of Animal thanks to super().

Static Methods

Static methods are class methods that can be called without creating an instance of the class.

```javascript
class Utilities {
  static sum(a, b) {
    return a + b;
  }

  static subtract(a, b) {
    return a - b;
  }
}

console.log(Utilities.sum(5, 3));  //  This will display 8
console.log(Utilities.subtract(10, 4));  //  This will display 6
```

Practice with Object-Oriented Programming

Now it's your turn to practice OOP in JavaScript:

- Create a class Product with properties like name, price, and a method showInfo() that displays the product information.

- Create a subclass Book that inherits from Product, with a new property author and a method showAuthor() that displays the author's name.

- Create objects of both classes and call their methods to verify their functionality.

Conclusion

In this chapter, we have explored Object-Oriented Programming in JavaScript:

- We learned how to define classes and create objects from them.

- We saw how to use constructors and methods in a class.

- We explored the concept of inheritance and how a class can inherit properties and methods from another.

- We saw how to use static methods in a class.

CHAPTER 9: SMALL PROJECTS

In this chapter, we will create three mini-projects to apply the knowledge acquired in JavaScript. The projects are: a Calculator, a To-Do List, and an Image Gallery. I will guide you step by step through each project so you can understand and build them.

Project 1: Calculator

In this project, we will create a basic calculator that can perform addition, subtraction, multiplication, and division operations.

Step 1: HTML Structure

Let's start by creating the basic HTML structure for our calculator.

```html
<!DOCTYPE html>
<html lang="en">
<head>

<meta charset="UTF-8">
  <title>Calculator</title>

<link rel="stylesheet" href="styles.css">
</head>

<body>

  <div class="calculator">
    <input type="text" id="result" disabled>
    <div class="buttons">
      <button onclick="clear()">C</button>
      <button onclick="addNumber(7)">7</button>
      <button onclick="addNumber(8)">8</button>
      <button onclick="addNumber(9)">9</button>
      <button onclick="addOperation('+')">+</button>
      <button onclick="addNumber(4)">4</button>
      <button onclick="addNumber(5)">5</button>
      <button onclick="addNumber(6)">6</button>
      <button onclick="addOperation('-')">-</button>
      <button onclick="addNumber(1)">1</button>
      <button onclick="addNumber(2)">2</button>
      <button onclick="addNumber(3)">3</button>
      <button onclick="addOperation('*')">*</button>
      <button onclick="addNumber(0)">0</button>
      <button onclick="addOperation('/')">/</button>
      <button onclick="calculateResult()">=</button>
    </div>
  </div>
```

```html
    <script src="script.js"></script>
</body>
</html>
```

Step 2: CSS Styles

We'll add some basic styles to make our calculator look better.

```css
body {
    font-family: Arial, sans-serif;
    background-color: #f5f5f5;
    display: flex;
    justify-content: center;
    align-items: center;
    height: 100vh;
    margin: 0;
}

.calculator {
    background-color: #fff;
    border-radius: 5px;
    box-shadow: 0 2px 10px rgba(0, 0, 0, 0.1);
    padding: 20px;
    width: 300px;
}

#result {
    width: calc(100% - 10px);
    margin-bottom: 10px;
    padding: 5px;
    font-size: 20px;
    border: 1px solid #ccc;
    border-radius: 3px;
```

```css
}
.buttons {
    display: grid;
    grid-template-columns: repeat(4, 1fr);
    grid-gap: 5px;
}

button {
    padding: 10px;
    font-size: 18px;
    border: 1px solid #ccc;
    border-radius: 3px;
    background-color: #f9f9f9;
    cursor: pointer;
}

button:hover {
    background-color: #e0e0e0;
}
```

Step 3: JavaScript

Now, let's create the script.js file to add the functionality of the calculator.

```javascript
let result = document.getElementById('result');
let operation = '';
let operand1 = '';
let operand2 = '';
let pendingOperation = false;
function clear() {
    result.value = '';
```

```
    operation = '';
    operand1 = '';
    operand2 = '';
    pendingOperation = false;
}

function addNumber(number) {
    if (pendingOperation) {
        result.value = '';
        pendingOperation = false;
    }
    result.value += number;
}

function addOperation(op) {
    operation = op;
    operand1 = parseFloat(result.value);
    pendingOperation = true;
}

function calculateResult() {
    if (operation !== '' && operand1 !== '' && result.value !== '') {
        operand2 = parseFloat(result.value);
        let finalResult = 0;
        switch (operation) {
            case '+':
                finalResult = operand1 + operand2;
                break;
            case '-':
                finalResult = operand1 - operand2;
                break;
            case '*':
                finalResult = operand1 * operand2;
                break;
            case '/':
                finalResult = operand1 / operand2;
```

```
        break;
    }
    result.value = finalResult;
    operation = '';
    operand1 = '';
    operand2 = '';
  }
}
```

Ready! Now you can open your HTML file in a browser, and you should see a functional calculator. You can perform basic addition, subtraction, multiplication, and division operations.

Project 2: To-Do List

In this project, we will create a simple To-Do List where users can add new tasks, mark them as completed, and delete them.

Step 1: HTML Structure

Let's start by creating the basic HTML structure for our To-Do List.

```html
<!DOCTYPE html>
<html lang="en">
<head>
    <meta charset="UTF-8">
    <title>To-Do List</title>
    <link rel="stylesheet" href="styles.css">
</head>
<body>

    <div class="todo">
        <h1>Task List</h1>
        <input type="text" id="newTask" placeholder="New task">
        <button onclick="addTask()">Add</button>
        <ul id="taskList">
            <!-- Tasks will be added here -->
        </ul>
    </div>
    <script src="script.js"></script>
</body>
</html>
```

Step 2: CSS Styles

We'll add some basic styles for our To-Do List.

```css
body {
  font-family: Arial, sans-serif;
  background-color: #f5f5f5;
  display: flex;
  justify-content: center;
  align-items: center;
  height: 100vh;
  margin: 0;
}

.todo {
  background-color: #fff;
  border-radius: 5px;
  box-shadow: 0 2px 10px rgba(0, 0, 0, 0.1);
  padding: 20px;
  width: 300px;
}

h1 {
  margin: 0 0 10px;
  font-size: 24px;
}

input[type="text"] {
  width: calc(100% - 10px);
  margin-bottom: 10px;
  padding: 5px;
  font-size: 16px;
  border: 1px solid #ccc;
  border-radius: 3px;
}
```

```css
button {
  padding: 10px;
  font-size: 16px;
  border: 1px solid #ccc;
  border-radius: 3px;
  background-color: #f9f9f9;
  cursor: pointer;
}

button:hover {
  background-color: #e0e0e0;
}

ul {
  list-style-type: none;
  padding: 0;
}

li {
  margin-bottom: 5px;
}

.completed {
  text-decoration: line-through;
  color: #aaa;
}
```

Step 3: JavaScript

Let's create the script.js file to add the functionality of the To-Do List.

```javascript
let newTask = document.getElementById('newTask');
let taskList = document.getElementById('taskList');

function addTask() {
  let taskText = newTask.value.trim();
  if (taskText !== '') {
    let taskElement = document.createElement('li');
    taskElement.innerText = taskText;
    taskElement.addEventListener('click', () => {
      taskElement.classList.toggle('completed');
    });
    taskList.appendChild(taskElement);
    newTask.value = '';
  }
}
```

Ready! Now you can open your HTML file in a browser, and you should see a functional To-Do List. You can add new tasks, mark them as completed by clicking on them, and delete them if you wish.

Project 3: Image Gallery

In this project, we will create a simple image gallery where users can view a selection of images and click on them to view them in full size.

Step 1: HTML Structure

Let's start by creating the basic HTML structure for our image gallery.

```html
<!DOCTYPE html>
<html lang="en">
<head>
    <meta charset="UTF-8">
    <title>Image Gallery</title>
    <link rel="stylesheet" href="styles.css">
</head>
<body>
    <div class="gallery">
        <h1>Image Gallery</h1>
        <div class="images">
            <img src="img/image1.jpg" alt="Image 1" onclick="openImage('img/image1.jpg')">
            <img src="img/image2.jpg" alt="Image 2" onclick="openImage('img/image2.jpg')">
            <img src="img/image3.jpg" alt="Image 3" onclick="openImage('img/image3.jpg')">
        </div>
        <div id="modal" class="modal">
            <span class="close" onclick="closeModal()">&times;</span>
            <img id="modalImage" src="" alt="Modal Image">
        </div>
```

```html
    </div>
    <script src="script.js"></script>
</body>
</html>
```

Step 2: CSS Styles

We'll add some basic styles for our image gallery.

```css
body {
    font-family: Arial, sans-serif;
    background-color: #f5f5f5;
    display: flex;
    justify-content: center;
    align-items: center;
    height: 100vh;
    margin: 0;
}

.gallery {
    background-color: #fff;
    border-radius: 5px;
    box-shadow: 0 2px 10px rgba(0, 0, 0, 0.1);
    padding: 20px;
    width: 600px;
}

h1 {
    margin: 0 0 20px;
    font-size: 24px;
}
```

```css
.images {
  display: grid;
  grid-template-columns: repeat(3, 1fr);
  grid-gap: 10px;
}

img {
  width: 100%;
  border-radius: 3px;
  cursor: pointer;
  transition: transform 0.3s;
}

img:hover {
  transform: scale(1.05);
}

.modal {
  display: none;
  position: fixed;
  z-index: 1;
  left: 0;
  top: 0;
  width: 100%;
  height: 100%;
  background-color: rgba(0, 0, 0, 0.7);
}

.modal img {
  display: block;
  margin: auto;
  max-width: 80%;
  max-height: 80%;
  cursor: pointer;
}

.close {
```

```
position: absolute;
top: 20px;
right: 20px;
font-size: 24px;
color: #fff;
cursor: pointer;
}
```

Step 3: JavaScript

Let's create the script.js file to add the functionality of the image gallery.

```javascript
let modal = document.getElementById('modal');
let modalImage = document.getElementById('modalImage');

function openImage(imagePath) {
   modal.style.display = 'block';
   modalImage.src = imagePath;
}

function closeModal() {
   modal.style.display = 'none';
}
```

Ready! Now you can open your HTML file in a browser, and you should see a functional image gallery. You can click on the images to view them in full size and close the modal by clicking on the "X".

Congratulations! You have completed the mini-projects of the Calculator, To-Do List, and Image Gallery in JavaScript. These projects allow you to apply the knowledge acquired and practice your programming skills.

CHAPTER 10: DEBUGGING AND BEST PRACTICES

In this chapter, we'll address debugging and some best practices of programming in JavaScript. We'll also discuss the importance of comments and code readability, version control with Git, and provide resources for further learning.

Debugging Tools

Debugging is the process of identifying and correcting errors in code. Here are some common tools that can assist you in debugging your JavaScript code:

Console.log()

console.log() is one of the simplest and most useful tools for printing messages and values to the browser console. You can use it to check the value of variables and the flow of your program.

Example:

```javascript
let name = "Juan";
console.log("The name is: ", name);
```

Browser DevTools

Most modern browsers come with integrated development tools, such as Chrome DevTools or Firefox Developer Tools. These tools allow you to inspect elements, debug JavaScript, monitor performance, and more.

You can open DevTools with:

- In Chrome: Right-click anywhere on the page and select "Inspect" or press Ctrl + Shift + I.

- In Firefox: Right-click anywhere on the page and select "Inspect Element" or press Ctrl + Shift + I.

Breakpoints (Puntos de Interrupción)

Breakpoints allow you to pause the execution of code at specific points and examine the state of variables at that moment. You can set breakpoints in DevTools by clicking on the line number where you want to pause.

Debugger Statement

The debugger statement is a way to set a breakpoint directly in your JavaScript code. When the JavaScript engine encounters this statement, it halts execution and opens the debugging tools if available.

Example:

```javascript
Copy code
function myFunction() {
    let x = 10;
    debugger; // The code stops here
    console.log(x);
}
```

Code Best Practices

Comments and Readability

Comments are parts of code that are not executed and are used to explain the purpose or functionality of the code. It's important to write clear and concise comments so that others can easily understand your code.

Example:

```javascript
// This function adds two numbers
function add(a, b) {
    return a + b;
}
```

In addition to comments, it's crucial to follow good readability practices:

- Use descriptive variable names.

- Format your code consistently.

- Use indentation and whitespace to improve readability.

Best Coding Practices

Avoiding Global Variables

It's a good practice to limit the use of global variables in your code. Global variables can cause namespace collision issues and make debugging difficult. Instead, use local variables or variables within functions whenever possible.

Example of local variables:

```javascript
function sum(a, b) {
    let result = a + b;
    return result;
}
```

Don't Repeat Yourself (DRY)

DRY stands for "Don't Repeat Yourself." Avoid repeating identical or similar code blocks. Instead, extract the repeated code into functions and reuse it in multiple places.

Example:

```javascript
// Bad: Code repetition
let name1 = "Juan";
console.log("Hola, " + name1);

let name2 = "María";
console.log("Hola, " + name2);

// Good: Using a function
function greet(name) {
    console.log("Hola, " + name);
}

greet("Juan");
greet("María");
```

Error Handling

It's always important to handle errors in your code to prevent your application from crashing or behaving unexpectedly.

Use try...catch blocks to capture and handle errors appropriately.

Example:

```javascript
try {
  // Code that may throw an error
  // ...
} catch (error) {
  // Error handling
  console.error("An error occurred:", error);
}
```

Version Control (Git)

Git is a widely used version control system that allows you to track changes to your code over time. Some basic Git concepts include:

Repository

A Git repository is a place where your code and its history of changes are stored. You can have a local repository on your machine and/or a remote repository on a cloud service like GitHub or GitLab.

Commits

A commit in Git is a snapshot of your changes at a specific point in time. Each commit has a descriptive message explaining the changes made.

Example of a commit:

```bash
git commit -m "Adding login functionality"
```

Branches

Branches in Git allow you to work on different versions of your code in isolation. You can create a new branch to develop a new feature without affecting the main branch (usually main or master).

Example of branch creation and switching:

```bash
git checkout -b new-functionality
```

Push and Pull

git push is used to send your local changes to a remote repository, while git pull is used to bring changes from the remote repository to your local repository.

Example of push and pull:

```bash
git push origin main
git pull origin main
```

Resources for Further Learning

- **Mozilla Developer Network (MDN):** Offers comprehensive and up-to-date documentation on JavaScript and its functionalities.

    o *Website: developer.mozilla.org*

- **FreeCodeCamp:** Free educational platform with interactive courses on JavaScript and web development.

    o *Website: freecodecamp.org*

- **JavaScript.info**: Modern and detailed tutorial on JavaScript, from basics to advanced topics.

    o *Website: javascript.info*

Conclusion

In this chapter, we've explored debugging tools, code best practices, the use of Git for version control, and resources for further learning JavaScript. It's crucial to adopt good practices from the beginning to write clean, readable code that's easy to maintain. Using Git will allow you to maintain a history of changes and collaborate effectively on projects.

CHAPTER 11: PUBLISHING AND DEPLOYMENT

In this chapter, we'll cover how to publish and deploy your JavaScript projects so they are available online. We'll discuss how to upload a project to GitHub, how to use a basic hosting service to showcase your project on the web, a brief introduction to JavaScript frameworks (optional), and some final tips.

Uploading a Project to GitHub

Step 1: Create a Repository on GitHub

1. Go to GitHub and create an account if you don't have one.

2. In the top right corner, click on the plus sign (+) and select "New repository."

3. Give your repository a name, add an optional

description, and choose whether you want it to be public or private.

4. Click on "Create repository."

Step 2: Upload Your Code

1. On your local machine, navigate to your project directory.

2. Initialize a Git repository with git init.

3. Add all files to the repository with git add.

4. Make your first commit with git commit -m "Initial commit."

5. Associate your remote repository with git remote add origin REPOSITORY_URL.

6. Push your code to the remote repository with git push -u origin main.

Basic Hosting

To showcase your project online, you can use basic hosting services like GitHub Pages or Netlify. Here's how to do it with GitHub Pages:

GitHub Pages

GitHub Pages is a free service that allows you to host static websites directly from a GitHub repository.

Step 1: Prepare Your Project

Ensure your project has a proper structure with HTML, CSS, and JavaScript files.

If you haven't already, create a gh-pages branch for your website.

```bash
git checkout -b gh-pages
```

Step 2: Upload Your Project to GitHub

- Follow the above steps to upload your project to GitHub.

- Make sure you are on the gh-pages branch.

- Push your code to the remote repository.

```bash
git push -u origin gh-pages
```

Step 3: Configure GitHub Pages

1. Go to your repository's settings page on GitHub.

2. Scroll down to the "GitHub Pages" section.

3. Select the gh-pages branch as the source and save.

4. Now your project should be available online at the URL https://yourusername.github.io/yourproject.

Final Tips

- **Practice Regularly:** Consistent practice is key to improving in programming.

- **Explore Documentation and Examples:** Official documentation and examples can be your best friends.

- **Participate in Communities:** Join online communities like Stack Overflow or Reddit to get help and learn from others.

Conclusion

In this chapter, we learned how to upload a project to GitHub, use GitHub Pages as a basic hosting service, and some final tips to improve in web development.

CHAPTER 12: EXPLORING JAVASCRIPT FRAMEWORKS

In this chapter, we'll explore the most popular JavaScript frameworks: React, Vue, and Angular. We'll start with a brief explanation of what a framework is and why you should consider using one. Then, we'll delve into each of the three frameworks, discussing their strengths, weaknesses, and why you might choose one over the others.

What is a Framework and Why Should You Use One?

A JavaScript framework is a tool that provides a structure and set of predefined tools to facilitate the development of web applications. Instead of having to write all the code from scratch, frameworks offer ready-made solutions for common tasks like state management, routing, DOM manipulation, and more.

Here are some reasons why you should consider using a framework:

- **Enhanced Productivity**: Frameworks offer a solid foundation and a set of built-in tools that can speed up the development process and make building complex applications easier.

- **Simplified Maintenance**: By following the framework's conventions and design patterns, your code will be more consistent and easier to maintain over time.

- **Active Community**: Popular frameworks often have a large community of developers who share knowledge, resources, and open-source libraries, which can be extremely helpful for problem-solving and improving your code.

- **Scalability**: Frameworks are designed to handle applications of any size, from small apps to large-scale enterprise projects.

React: The Library for Building User Interfaces

React is a JavaScript library developed by Facebook used to build interactive and dynamic user interfaces. Here are some of its key features:

Strengths:

- **Virtual DOM**: React uses a Virtual DOM to enhance performance and efficiency of DOM updates, resulting in a faster user experience.

- **Component-Based**: React follows a component-based development approach, making code reuse and modular interface creation easier.

- **Large Community**: React has a large community of developers who contribute libraries, tools, and resources, making learning and problem-solving easier.

Weaknesses:

- **Steep Learning Curve:** For those new to React, the learning curve can be steep, especially for those unfamiliar with the component-based development paradigm.

Why Choose React?:

If you're building an application with a complex user interface that needs to handle frequent updates and efficient rendering, React is an excellent choice. Its focus on component development and Virtual DOM make it ideal for dynamic and highly interactive applications.

Vue: The Lightweight and Versatile Alternative

Vue.js is a progressive JavaScript framework used to build interactive and dynamic user interfaces.

Developed by Evan You, Vue has rapidly gained popularity due to its simplicity, flexibility, and gentle learning curve.

Here's why you might choose Vue.js for your next project:

Strengths:

- **Gentle Learning Curve:** Vue.js is known for its gentle learning curve, making it a great choice for those new to web development.

- **Flexibility:** Vue.js is a progressive framework, meaning you can use as much or as little of it as you like in your project. You can gradually integrate it into existing projects or start from scratch.

- **Efficient Performance:** Vue.js uses an efficient reactivity system that minimizes DOM changes and maximizes application performance.

- **Clear and Concise Documentation:** Vue.js has clear and concise documentation that makes learning and quick reference easy.

Weaknesses:

- **Community Size:** While Vue.js has an active and growing community, its size may not be as large as React or Angular, leading to limited availability of resources and libraries.

Why Choose Vue.js?:

If you're looking for a lightweight, easy-to-learn, and highly flexible framework for building interactive web applications, Vue.js is an excellent choice. Its developer-focused approach, gentle learning curve, and efficient performance make it ideal for projects of any size.

Angular: The Comprehensive and Robust Framework

Angular is a web application development framework developed by Google. It's a popular choice for building complex and scalable web applications.

Here's why you might choose Angular for your next project:

Strengths:

- **MVC Architecture:** Angular follows a Model-View-Controller (MVC) architecture, making it easy to organize and structure application code.

- **Dependency Injection:** Angular has a built-in dependency injection system that makes component creation and testing easier.

- **Optimized Performance:** Angular uses advanced performance optimization techniques like change detection and one-way data binding to ensure optimal performance even in complex applications.

- **Angular CLI:** Angular CLI is a command-line tool that simplifies the development, testing, and deployment process of Angular applications.

Weaknesses:

- **Steep Learning Curve:** Angular has a steep learning curve, especially for those new to web development or with experience with simpler frameworks like React or Vue.js.

- **Complexity:** For small projects or simple applications, Angular may be too complex and overly burdensome for development.

Why Choose Angular?:

If you're building a large and complex application that requires a solid architecture, optimized performance, and a comprehensive set of features, Angular is an excellent choice. Its focus on modularity, code organization, and scalable development practices make it ideal for enterprise and large-scale projects.

In Summary

- **React:** Ideal for dynamic and interactive applications with a focus on component development and efficient DOM updates.

- **Vue:** A lightweight and easy-to-learn option for building interactive web applications with a gentle learning curve and great flexibility.

- **Angular:** Perfect for large projects that require a solid architecture, optimized performance

Each of these frameworks has its own strengths and weaknesses, and the choice depends on the type of project you're building and your personal preferences.

APPENDIX: PRACTICAL EXERCISES

Here are a series of practical exercises designed to review and consolidate the concepts learned in this book on JavaScript programming from scratch. Put yourself to the test and continue improving your skills!

- **Exercise 1: Variables and Operators**

    1. Declare two variables, numero1 and numero2, and initialize them with numeric values.

    2. Perform the following operations using the declared variables: addition, subtraction, multiplication, division, and modulus.

    3. Print the result of each operation to the console.

- **Exercise 2: Conditionals**

    1. Declare a variable called edad and initialize it with a numerical value.

2. Use a conditional structure to determine if the person is of legal age (18 years or older) or not.

3. Print a message to the console indicating whether the person is of legal age or not.

- **Exercise 3: Loops**

    1. Use a for loop to print the numbers from 1 to 10 to the console.

    2. Use a while loop to print the numbers from 1 to 10 to the console.

- **Exercise 4: Functions**

    1. Create a function called calcularAreaRectangulo that takes two parameters, base and hight, and returns the area of the rectangle (base * hight).

    2. Call the function with specific values for base and hight and print the result to the console.

- **Exercise 5: Arrays**

    1. Declare an array called nombres that contains several names of people.

    2. Use a for loop to print each name in the array to the console.

- **Exercise 6: Objects**

    1. Create an object called persona with the following properties: nombre, edad, and ciudad.

    2. Print each property of the object to the console.

- **Exercise 7: DOM Manipulation**

    1. Create an HTML file with a button and an empty paragraph.

    2. Use JavaScript to add an event to the button that changes the text of the paragraph to "Hello, world!" when the button is clicked.

- **Exercise 8: Advanced DOM Manipulation**

    1. Modify the previous exercise so that, instead of changing the text of the paragraph, a new paragraph is added to the document with the text "Hello, world!" when the button is clicked.

- **Exercise 9: Final Project**

    1. Choose a small project and try to implement it on your own using the concepts learned in this book.

    2. If you feel confident, try to enhance and expand your project by adding new functionalities.

GLOSSARY

- **JavaScript**: A high-level programming language mainly used for adding interactivity to web pages.

- **HTML (HyperText Markup Language)**: The standard markup language used to create web pages and web applications.

- **CSS (Cascading Style Sheets)**: A language used to describe the style and presentation of HTML documents.

- **Framework**: A defined support structure in which other software can be organized and developed.

- **Virtual DOM**: A memory representation of a DOM (Document Object Model) tree that allows for efficient updates to the actual DOM.

- **Component**: A reusable, modular part of a user interface that encapsulates functionality and styling.

- **Learning Curve**: The time and effort required to learn and master a new technology or concept.

- **DOM (Document Object Model)**: A hierarchical representation of HTML or XML documents that allows interaction with the structure and content of a web page.

- **Progressive Framework**: A framework that can be adopted gradually, allowing developers to add only the features they need.

- **Dependency Injection**: A design pattern where an

object's dependencies are supplied from the outside rather than created internally.

- **CLI (Command Line Interface)**: A command-line interface that allows users to interact with a program using text commands.

- **Performance**: The speed and efficiency with which an application or system performs a task.

- **Modularity**: The principle of dividing a program into separate modules that are easier to develop, maintain, and reuse.

- **SPA (Single Page Application)**: A web application that loads a single HTML page and dynamically updates content as the user interacts with the application.

- **Git**: A distributed version control system used to track changes in source code during software development.

- **Firebase**: A mobile and web application development platform developed by Google that provides a variety of cloud services, including Firebase Authentication.

- **GitHub**: A web-based source code hosting platform that uses Git for version control and collaboration on software projects.

- **Hosting**: The process of storing and making a website or web application accessible on a remote server.

- **DOM Manipulation**: The ability to modify the structure and content of an HTML document using JavaScript.

- **Component-Oriented Framework**: A framework that relies on creating and reusing components as the basic unit of development.

- **Angular CLI**: A command-line interface that facilitates the development, testing, and deployment of Angular applications.

- **Performance Optimization**: The process of improving the performance of a web application through techniques such as efficient code and fast resource loading.

- **React Native**: A mobile application development framework that allows developers to build native apps using React and JavaScript.

- **Vue CLI**: A command-line tool for developing Vue.js applications that simplifies project setup and deployment.

- **Community**: A group of people who share common interests and support each other in pursuing similar goals.

www.ingramcontent.com/pod-product-compliance
Lightning Source LLC
Chambersburg PA
CBHW070156230526
45471CB00002B/688